What's the Issue?

WHAT'S INTOLERANCE?

By Richard Alexander

KidHaven
PUBLISHING

Published in 2018 by
KidHaven Publishing, an Imprint of Greenhaven Publishing, LLC
353 3rd Avenue
Suite 255
New York, NY 10010

Designer: Deanna Paternostro
Editor: Katie Kawa

Photo Credits: Cover (top) © istockphoto.com/monkeybusinessimages; cover (bottom) © istockphoto.com/SoumenNath; p. 4 iofoto/Shutterstock.com; pp. 5, 6, 17, 21 Rawpixel.com/ Shutterstock.com; p. 7 sirtravelalot/Shutterstock.com; p. 8 Robert Kneschke/Shutterstock.com; p. 9 SpeedKingz/Shutterstock.com; p. 11 a katz/Shutterstock.com; p. 12 Ms Jane Campbell/ Shutterstock.com; p. 13 Kdonmuang/Shutterstock.com; p. 14 Daniel M Ernst/Shutterstock.com; p. 15 RabbitHolePhoto/Shutterstock.com; p. 19 s_maria/Shutterstock.com.

Cataloging-in-Publication Data

Names: Alexander, Richard.
Title: What's intolerance? / Richard Alexander.
Description: New York : KidHaven Publishing, 2018. | Series: What's the issue? | Includes glossary and index.
Identifiers: ISBN 9781534525078 (pbk.) | 9781534524392 (library bound) | ISBN 9781534525085 (6 pack) | ISBN 9781534524408 (ebook)
Subjects: LCSH: Toleration–Juvenile literature. | Equality–Juvenile literature. | Racism–Juvenile literature. | Discrimination–Juvenile literature.
Classification: LCC HM1271.R64 2018 | DDC 305–dc23

Printed in the United States of America

CPSIA compliance information: Batch #CW18KL: For further information contact Greenhaven Publishing LLC, New York, New York at 1-844-317-7404.

Please visit our website, www.greenhavenpublishing.com. For a free color catalog of all our high-quality books, call toll free 1-844-317-7404 or fax 1-844-317-7405.

CONTENTS

Differences All Around Us

The world is made up of many different kinds of people. All around us are people with different beliefs, people who speak different languages, people of different races, and people who come from different countries. No two people are exactly alike!

Many people believe these differences should be celebrated and that we have a lot to learn from each other. However, some people don't like those they see as different. They want everyone to be the same. This way of thinking is called intolerance. It's important to fight against intolerance to make everyone feel welcome and accepted.

Facing the Facts

More than half of all Americans who took part in a 2016 study said they think having many different kinds of people in their country makes it a better place to live.

We can learn a lot by getting to know people who are different from us. This is a good way to fight intolerance.

The Roots of Intolerance

Intolerance can come in many forms. Some people don't like others because they look different, while other people show intolerance toward people of different **religious** beliefs. In addition, people can sometimes be intolerant of those who think differently than they do.

Where does intolerance come from? For many people, intolerance has its roots in fear. People are often afraid of what they don't know or understand. It's easier to think of people who are different as bad and scary than to listen to and learn from each other. Learning helps people become more tolerant, or accepting of differences.

Intolerant people see different opinions or ideas as wrong instead of as another way of thinking.

Facing the Facts

One of the most important groups fighting intolerance around the world is the United Nations Educational, Scientific and Cultural Organization, which is also known as UNESCO.

What Are Stereotypes?

People look for easy and fast ways to group other people together. They often do this using stereotypes. These are ideas people have about all the members of one group, such as a race, religion, or **political** party. Stereotypes are often overly simple and sometimes completely untrue.

Intolerant people often believe stereotypes and use those stereotypes to explain why they don't like people from certain groups. This is why getting to know people as individuals and not stereotypes is such an important part of fighting intolerance.

Facing the Facts

British scientists discovered that the human brain **reacts** more strongly to negative stereotypes than positive facts about people.

Stereotypes can often lead to prejudice, which is a bad feeling a person has about someone else that's not based in facts. Prejudices form when people judge others before getting to know them.

Intolerance Toward Immigrants

Different groups have faced intolerance throughout history. Immigrants have often been the **victims** of intolerance. An immigrant is someone who comes to another country to live there. Immigrants are often trying to build a better life for themselves and their families. However, some people are afraid of immigrants. They think immigrants are going to take their jobs.

People who show intolerance toward immigrants often dislike the **customs** they bring with them from their home country. Instead of learning about people from different **cultures**, intolerant people believe all immigrants should blend in or go back to where they came from.

Although immigrants continue to face intolerance in the countries they move to, many people have joined together to speak out against this kind of intolerance.

WE ARE IMMIGRANTS HERE TOSTAY

WE ARE MOTHERS FATHERS CHILDREN STAY

MIGRATION IS A HUMAN RIGHT

Facing the Facts 🔍

According to a 2016 study, 45 percent of Americans believe immigration hurts American workers, while 42 percent believe it helps American workers.

Religious Intolerance

Some immigrants also face intolerance because their religious beliefs are different from those of the people around them. Even people who aren't immigrants sometimes struggle with religious intolerance.

Jewish people have often been treated poorly because of their religious beliefs and their **unique** culture. Today, Muslims, or people who practice the religion of Islam, are often the victims of intolerance. Some **terrorist** attacks have been carried out by people who claim to follow Islam but aren't supported by other Muslims. Their actions have caused some people to believe all Muslims are terrorists, which isn't true.

Fight against racism and Islamophobia

STAND UP TO RACISM

SAY NO TO ISLAMOPHOBIA!

12

Facing the Facts 🔍

Islamophobia is fear or dislike shown toward Muslims.

Many Muslim women and girls choose to wear a covering for their hair called a hijab. Some intolerant people believe they shouldn't be allowed to wear a hijab and have even tried to pull them off the heads of Muslim women.

Political Problems

Different ways of thinking can often lead to good **debates** where people learn from each other. However, they can also lead to **division** between groups of people who don't agree with each other. People are sometimes intolerant of different ideas or opinions. They believe their way of thinking is the right way, so people who disagree must be wrong.

In the United States, there are different political parties made up of people with different ideas about how the government should work. Members of one party often view members of the other party as intolerant.

14

Facing the Facts 🔍

As of 2016, more than half of the members of the two main political parties in the United States—the Democratic Party and the Republican Party—had a negative view of the other party.

Sharing different ideas can often make the world a better place. However, when people are intolerant, they react angrily to different ways of thinking.

Other Examples of Intolerance

There are many other forms of intolerance that people face in the world today. When people make fun of someone with a disability or someone who speaks a different language, they're being intolerant. People also show intolerance when they're unable to accept all kinds of families, such as families with two moms, two dads, or parents of different races.

Intolerance can also be seen when people try to keep those who are different from getting certain jobs or going to certain schools. This is called discrimination.

Facing the Facts

Intolerance toward same-sex marriages has gone down in recent years. In a 2010 poll, 42 percent of Americans said they supported same-sex marriage, but that number rose to 62 percent by 2017.

The world is becoming more diverse, which means it's filled with people who are different from each other. Intolerant people think that's a bad thing, but most people believe it's a good thing.

Words and Actions

Intolerance is often shown with words, but sometimes it's shown in actions. Intolerant governments can **deny** certain groups basic rights because they're different. Intolerance can also turn **violent**.

Intolerance isn't a crime, but it can lead people to **commit** crimes. Hate crimes are illegal acts committed because of intolerance and prejudice. These crimes are often violent and happen when someone wants to hurt another person because they're different. The number of hate crimes in the United States has risen in recent years, but groups such as the Southern Poverty Law Center are working hard to end violent intolerance.

Facing the Facts

A hate group is a group that practices intolerance—often in a violent way. As of 2017, there were more than 900 hate groups in the United States.

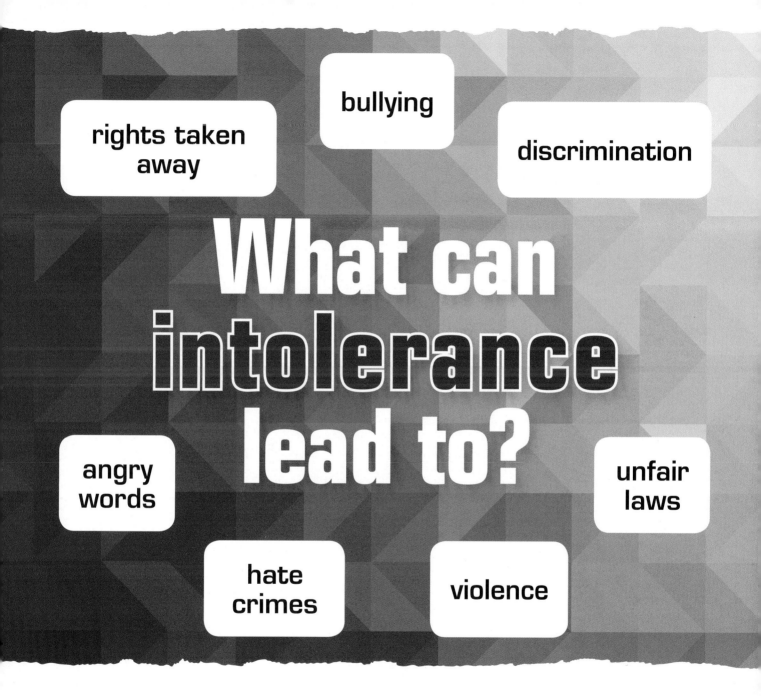

rights taken
away

bullying

discrimination

What can intolerance lead to?

angry
words

unfair
laws

hate
crimes

violence

Intolerance can lead to hurtful words and harmful actions. It may be a big problem, but every small action counts in the fight against it.

Building a More Tolerant World

Intolerance can be seen anywhere—from governments and schools to homes and the Internet. Fighting intolerance starts with noticing times when you thought or acted in an intolerant way. It's important to learn from those times and to try to be more accepting of people in the future.

The best way to fight intolerance is with understanding and respect. When people think or act differently than you do, learn the reasons why instead of deciding right away that they're wrong. When people learn to respect each other's differences instead of fearing them, the world becomes a more tolerant place.

Facing the Facts

Scientists believe children become aware of differences between groups of people and can start forming prejudices as early as 3 years old.

20

WHAT CAN YOU DO?

If you see someone being picked on for being different, tell an adult.

Speak out against intolerance when you hear people saying unkind things.

Raise money for local or national groups that work to end intolerance and hate crimes.

Read about different cultures, religions, and ways of thinking.

Make friends with people who are different from you, and learn about their lives.

If you disagree with someone, talk to them respectfully about their point of view.

These are just some of the things you can do to fight against intolerance. How will you help spread tolerance in your school, your home, and your community?

GLOSSARY

commit: To do something—often something that is wrong.

culture: The beliefs and ways of life of a certain group of people.

custom: An action or way of behaving that is traditional among the people in a certain group or place.

debate: An argument or discussion about an issue, generally between two sides.

deny: To refuse to grant.

division: Separation.

political: Relating to government and beliefs about how governments should work.

react: To behave in a certain way when something happens.

religious: Relating to a set of beliefs about a god or gods.

terrorist: Having to do with using violence and fear as a way to achieve a political goal.

unique: Special or different from anything else.

victim: A person who is hurt by someone else.

violent: Relating to the use of bodily force to hurt others.

FOR MORE INFORMATION

WEBSITES

Stand Up for Someone's Rights Today
www.standup4humanrights.org/en/
Visitors to this website learn more about a worldwide effort to stand up for human rights, spread respect, and fight intolerance.

Teaching Tolerance: Mix It Up
www.tolerance.org/mix-it-up
This website offers information on how your school can participate in Mix It Up at Lunch Day, which is a day for students to sit with someone new at lunch to help make schools more tolerant places.

BOOKS

Hanson, Anders. *Everyone Is Equal: The Kids' Book of Tolerance.* Minneapolis, MN: ABDO Publishing Company, 2015.

Payne, Lauren Murphy, and Melissa Iwai. *We Can Get Along: A Child's Book of Choices.* Minneapolis, MN: Free Spirit Publishing, 2015.

Sullivan-Simon, Stacie, and Chad Thompson. *I Am Me & You Are You.* San Antonio, TX: Halo Publishing International, 2017.

INDEX